Manchest
FRAME *by* FRAME

CW00351142

Belle Vue	04
Growing Up	12
Whit Walks	20
Derby Days	28
Hospitals	38
Pope's Visit	44
Free Trade Hall	52
Moss Side	60
Travel	68
Modern Manchester	74

Welcome to Manchester: Frame by Frame, an 84-page publication crammed full of evocative and real-life images of a time many of us remember with warmth, fondness and fascination.

In this book you will see photographs which will immediately transport you back to a time of pounds, shillings and pence; of corner shops, cobbled streets and donkey stones.

The Whit Walks were magical events like no other. With new shoes that rubbed, new shirts too starched or new skirts too long we would seek out aunties and grandmas hoping they would notice our pristine outfit and cross our outstretched palm with a threepenny bit or even a silver tanner.

We probably did not really appreciate how lucky we were to have Belle Vue on our doorstep. We would watch our favourite performers in the Free Trade hall, perhaps not appreciating the significance of the location and the name of the venue. And only now, with the passage of time, do we properly celebrate the fact that Bevin's brand-new NHS was born here.

We take pride in the way we dominate football, hosting two of the most famous clubs in the world. Some of the notorious battles between City and United are documented here. We also mark today's cityscape – a skyline of shiny glass buildings proudly announcing Manchester's ambition for the future.

This book is about our the legacy of our lives, our families and our communities. All of it recognisable and still strangely relevant.

Eamonn O'Neal
Managing Editor, Manchester Evening News

Heritage Editor: Harri Aston
Written by: Eamonn O'Neal
Picture research: Sheenah Alcock
Designer: Ben Renshaw

Part of the Lost Britain **Collection**
© 2013 Trinity Mirror. All Rights Reserved

Managing Director: Ken Rogers
Senior Editor: Steve Hanrahan
Senior Art Editor: Rick Cooke
Editor: Paul Dove
Senior Marketing Executive: Claire Brown
Photosales: 0845 300 3021
Images: Mirrorpix, PA Photos
Printed by: William Gibbons

The circus ring at Belle Vue's Kings Hall performance before the complex is

Vue to a thrill at the city's big attraction

It had a zoo, a circus, an amusement park and attracted a host of international stars, so it's easy to see how Belle Vue became loved by thousands for its magical blend of entertainment

▲ **All the fun of the fair** Belle Vue's fun fair during the August bank holiday in August 1949

IN the early 1800s a parcel of land previously used for the digging of lime was leased for commercial use. It was a prime location adjacent to Hyde Road in Gorton and, in 1834, businessman William Crisp announced he was opening "Belle Vue Tea Gardens".

Two years later a visionary entrepreneur, John Jennison, took out a 99-year lease, added a lake and a natural history museum, thus extending the gardens by approximately 13 acres.

During the following 10 years a maze was created in the gardens, a racecourse built and the famous Hyde Road entrance was constructed. Famed for its fireworks displays and huge ballroom, the innovations at Belle Vue just kept on coming.

Brass band competitions, its own railway station, Italian gardens, hotel and even a brewery sprang up over the years.

Belle Vue became renowned for its zoo and, in 1873, the first elephant house was built to accommodate Maharajah – a fine animal purchased for £680 from one of the Wombwell's Travelling Menageries.

The plan was to transport Maharajah from Edinburgh by train but the elephant famously smashed through his railway truck. A revised plan

saw Maharajah walk from Scotland to Manchester with his trainer Lorenzo Lawrence, a journey that took 10 days. Lions, sea-lions, monkeys and camels soon followed and in order to look after the animals efficiently, and to become eco-friendly before the term was even invented, Belle Vue began generating its own electricity.

That also paved the way for further innovative developments including The King's Hall, an athletics ground and a roller-skating rink. The famous amusement park followed and the people of Manchester were treated to rides such as The Bobs, Helter Skelter Lighthouse, Scenic Railway and the Figure of Eight Toboggan Ride.

The most notable development for Belle Vue came in 1929 with the introduction of speedway and the Christmas circus. The speedway team is still going strong but the final curtain came down on the circus in January 1982.

When you throw in major wrestling tournaments and concerts featuring a host of international stars – including Jimi Hendrix, The Rolling Stones and The Who – it is easy to see how Belle Vue, after humble beginnings, became loved by thousands of people for its unique, magical blend of animals, activities and entertainment.

Head for heights Workmen check over the new giant water chute built at Belle Vue on April 17, 1957. Our camera gives the view that the passengers had as they started their exciting and exhilarating descent into the water

▲ **Water laugh** The opening of the new water chute at Belle Vue on April 19, 1957. Among the people in the car for its first run were Belle Vue managing director Sir Leslie Joesph, speedway rider Dick Fisher, his wife Jean, retired speedway star Ken Sharples and publicity manager Johnny Hoskins, who lost his hat on the ride

▲ **Scream time** Thrill-seekers on a roller-coaster at Belle Vue in August 1946

▶ **Popular attraction** Visitors at Belle Vue during the Easter of 1969

◀ **Stripe-tease!** Just because she's a cross between a tiger and a lioness this glamour puss thinks she's the cat's whiskers. She was called Tigon, pictured in August 1957, and was bred by the Sultan of Morocco. When she arrived at Belle Vue's zoo she was believed to be the only one in Britain

▼ **Monkeying around** Poor old Topaz wasn't the same chimpanzee after her keeper took her for a stroll around the amusement centre at Belle Vue because the animal decided to chance her luck on a fruit machine – and became hooked. Every day she would pester her keepers to take her back to play the one-armed bandit. This photograph was taken in February 1976

Height of good living Hilda, one of the giraffes that was brought over from Africa to Belle Vue, is enticed into its new home in June 1960

▼ **Specs appeal** Capi the monkey gets an eye-full as he plays with a pair of glasses in October 1972

◀ **Way to go** Children get a lift and an unusual experience to remember thanks to a willing elephant in May 1957

Pull the other one Topaz the chimp pulls the tail of Luke, a Leopard cub in May 1976. The two youngsters were big attractions at Belle Vue's zoo

▲ **Bye bye ducky** Lisa Kay says goodbye to Pip, her pet white duck. Lisa decided to donate Pip to Belle Vue's zoo on September 3, 1968

Trunk call Children feeding very happy-looking elephants at the Elephant House in August 1970

▶ *Jumpers for goalposts* Children playing football on the streets of Manchester in May 1967

Golden childhood of post-war era

Care-free days spent playing on cobbled streets until the sun went down, the roads and alleys became an open playground for children

Like many towns and cities in England, the people of post-war Manchester faced up to rebuilding their lives against a backdrop of austerity.

Although times were undeniably difficult, the children did not seem to notice and the streets were their playgrounds. There was hardly any traffic so the narrow roads held little danger as heavy, leather footballs were kicked against kerbstones and two-a-ball contests bounced off gable ends.

Cobbles were no hindrance to inventive skipping games and swinging on an old gas lamp never did anyone any harm. Children stayed out all day and parents did not fret.

The phrase environment-friendly had not been invented, yet mothers everywhere recycled clothes through the many layers of extended family and friends, socks were darned and bath water was shared.

In schools following the war, as well as the usual subjects, children were taught about road safety and first-aid. In those days teachers were renowned for being extremely strict and used corporal punishment to instil discipline, smacking and using canes, straps, slippers and rulers. A lot of teaching was done by rote – learning things by repetition, such as times tables.

Teaching was not structured in the way it is today but standards were checked by Her Majesty's Inspectors, who paid regular visits to all schools. As a rule the school day started at 9am and finished at 4pm. PE was called Physical Training and lessons were spent either hanging from wall-bars in the school hall or shivering on an uneven field in all weathers.

Typical school dinners in the 1950s were designed to be simple and filling. They would include meat and two veg, macaroni cheese and fish followed by semolina, tapioca, rice-pudding or, on special occasions, sponge and custard.

▲ *Hanging around* Pupils at Littlemoss High School, in Droylsden, receive some physical education

The caring kind *A Plymouth Grove School pupil shows her caring side in Piccadilly, alongside The Queen Victoria Monument, in 1945*

▲ **Unhappy landings** *A toddler in a Manchester department store is upset by the doves in Santa's Grotto when one lands on her head in December 1954*

▲ **Beach baby** One-year-old Alison Smith, from Cheetham Hill in Manchester, enjoying the pleasures of the beach for the first time in her life at Blackpool in May 1953

◀ **Fun in the snow** *January 1960 and 10-month-old Susan Torkington gets a tow on the snow-clad slopes of Lyme Park from her three-year-old sister, Linda*

15

▲ **Star batsman**
*Manchester
United legend
George Best
enjoys a game of
street cricket in
Chorlton-cum-
Hardy with some
local school
children in May
1968*

◀ **Safe streets**
*Children playing
in the streets of
Oldham in July
1952*

Swinging Britain Children in a Manchester street find their own enjoyment in March 1943 with the aid of a rope and a lamp post

◀ **Simple pleasures** Football legends Bobby Charlton, Sir Matt Busby and Derek Dougan playing football in the street with children in November 1970

Narrow streets Children enjoy a warm day in July 1952 when the front doors were left open and there were plenty of people around

▶ *Tough times*
The immediate
post-war period
was hard for
the country but
these children
in Manchester
seem oblivious
to their
surroundings in
February 1947

▲ *At least it's warm* These children,
pictured in February 1947, had no
such luxury as their own room – they
even had to share a bed

◀ *City under siege* Manchester
children warm themselves by a brazier
following an air raid on the city in
March 1941

Slum shame In the early 1970s it was claimed Salford had the worst slums in Europe. Here, five-year-old Jeffrey Slean "comes out to play" after school, watched by his mother, Vera Slean, in October 1974

▲ **School days** Facilities were minimal but the learning still went on in this Manchester school during the cold February of 1947

Out with the old A young boy dressed as a cowboy stares out at the newly-built tower blocks that rise above the old cobbled streets of Manchester in the 1960s

Miles of smiles Manchester Whit Walks is a much-loved city tradition

Step right along for the Whit Walks

A long-held and much-loved tradition has been a rite of passage for many youngsters in the city, with mums, dads, grandmothers and grandads proudly watching on

It is an annual tradition which stretches back more than 200 years – and it is still going strong. Thousands don their Sunday best and take to the streets for the Whit Walks,

At the height of their popularity, 30,000 people from church groups, schools, cultural organisations and associations gathered to parade around the streets.

Scholars have traced the first 'walks' to around 1800, arising from the Sunday School movement which began in 1784.

When Whitsuntide became an annual holiday during the 19th century, the mills would shut down and the workers could enjoy the celebrations. They would perhaps take a trip on the canals or later the railways.

In Manchester, children traditionally gathered in St Ann's Square but the focus was later changed to Albert Square. There, each school or group would have been allocated a space to congregate, marked by fluttering flags. The walkers would arrive against a backdrop of musicians tuning up and banners being unfurled.

The clergy, dressed in their ceremonial finery, would be holding court, ready to lead out each section. The groups would leave the square marching, straight-backed, behind their nominated band to be cheered through the city's streets by throngs of sightseers on pavements and office window sills. One exciting by-product for the children of the time is the money they had collected by appearing, hand outstretched, in front of their aunties and grandmas showing off their smart, starched new clothes.

▲ **Helping hand**
Whit Walkers in Manchester's Albert Square, June 11,1962

Musical youth *Two girls try their hand at the trombone and cymbals, 1960*

All smiles *Two young friends taking part in the June 1960 Whit Walks*

Tremendous trio *These three enjoy the 1960 celebrations*

On the move *Youngsters from the O'Neal School of Irish Dancing, pictured in the early 1960s, who walked behind Wythenshawe's Fianna Phadraig Pipe Band every year*

▲ **Walk the dog**
The little girl who brought her dog along to walk in the Whit Walks of June 1960 was three-year-old Diane Pugh. With her is Anne Grimley aged 11 and, of course, Judy the Yorkshire terrier

▶ **Spectators gather** The crowds enjoy the crackling atmosphere in June 1960

▲ **In costume** *Period silks for brother and sister Peter and Kelley Rooney, walking with St Cuthbert's Church members in Miles Platting in May 1986*

March of time *A young boy dressed as a soldier enjoys his ice cream cone after the walk in 1960*

Tuning up *On the march in Miles Platting in 1986*

Heavy load *Members of the Manchester Italian Catholic Society walk through Manchester in 1988*

Iconic An Italian Society group carrying a statue of the Madonna and Child during the Whit Walks in Manchester in the 1930s

Early walk Whit walkers in central Manchester, circa 1910

▶ **Flying the flag** *A scene from the Whit Walks of 1983*

▼ **Great day** *The procession makes its way through Manchester in 1986*

▼ **Busy streets** *Walkers are photographed taking part in the event in 1994*

▶ **Derby clash** Manchester City keeper Bert Trautmann collects from Manchester United's Tommy Taylor at Maine Road during this FA Cup match, which City won 2-0, on January 29, 1955

Derby days made in heaven or hell

Clashes between Manchester's two giants can lay claim to being among the most historic and dramatic in football, with a wealth of legends contesting the fixture

The Manchester derbies are arguably the most fiercely contested games in the English league – although before the Second World War many fans supported both clubs equally enthusiastically.

Following the war, dedication to one or other club became more common and colours were very definitely nailed to the mast.

In the first competitive derby since 1939, more than 71,000 fans flooded Maine Road. In the return match – also at Maine Road with United's ground out of action due to bomb damage – 71,690 supporters came to the game, a league record for derby games at Maine Road.

Sadly, the game failed to live up to expectations with United, who went on to win the FA Cup that year, holding City to a 0-0 draw.

In the December 1970 derby, a tackle by George Best broke the leg of Glyn Pardoe. The following season, during a 3–3 draw, a couple of legends clashed.

Francis Lee accused George Best of diving. Lee made his point to the referee by throwing himself to the floor.

Two great stalwarts were sent off in the first derby of the 1973-1974 season. Mike Doyle and Lou Macari were each shown a red card. They refused to leave the pitch, and the referee took both teams back to the dressing room until Doyle and Macari accepted their dismissal.

The return fixture at Old Trafford that season has become known as the Denis Law derby. On 81 minutes Colin Bell found Francis Lee who passed to Law, who had his back to the goal. Improvising, the Lawman back-heeled the ball beyond keeper Alex Stepney.

Delighted team-mates went to congratulate him but knowing United faced relegation, Law walked off the pitch with his head bowed.

The game continued for a few minutes until a pitch invasion by United fans forced the referee to blow for full time, with the result standing at 1-0 to City. It proved to be The Lawman's last touch in league football.

▲ *Maine event*
Tommy Taylor tries a header but is thwarted by City's Ken Barnes as Sky Blues captain Roy Paul looks on. City won the game 2-0 in February 1955

◀ **Sixties star**
Manchester
United star
Nobby Stiles
during a training
session before
the upcoming
derby match in
December 1969

▶ **Legendary
names** Roger
Byrne and
Duncan Edwards
of Manchester
United watch Don
Revie head the
ball to one of his
colleagues during
the 1955 FA Cup
game

Day of destiny A goal-mouth scramble during the famous derby clash that saw United relegated in April 1974 at Old Trafford

City joy, United woe Fans invade the pitch and swamp goalscorer, and former United player, Denis Law as United head towards relegation

▲ Anxious moments *As the drama of United's failed relegation survival bid unfolds the rival managers look on, Tony Book (right) of Manchester City and Tommy Docherty (left) of United*

◀ Trouble brews *The fans begin to encroach onto the pitch*

◀ Post-match chaos *The City players head down the Old Trafford tunnel, leaving the fans and police on the pitch*

▶ **Derby return**
The team captains, Manchester United's Johnny Carey (right) and Eric Westwood (left) of Man City, shake hands before the derby game on September 20, 1947. The game was a drab, goalless draw but was only the third meeting between the teams since 1931 and the first after the Second World War

▶ **Packing the crowd** Maine Road witnessed a record derby crowd on September 20, 1947, as 78,000 people packed into the ground

Manchester United players George Best, Nobby Stiles, Brian Kidd and Bobby Charlton finish training at Old Trafford before the Manchester derby in December 1969

Missing out Manchester City legend Colin Bell, who was unfit for the big derby match with Manchester United, spends a few minutes at Old Trafford in December 1969

Champagne era A league clash at Old Trafford on Wednesday, March 27, 1968. City won 3-1 and went on to win the league championship, while United clinched the European Cup at Wembley

▲ **Taken off** A player is carried off the field during the derby match at Old Trafford on Wednesday March 27,1968, when a 3-1 win for City went a long way to help secure the league title

◄ **Manchester legends** The two great Manchester football managers came face to face on the eve of the second leg of the League Cup played at Old Trafford on December 17, 1969. Joe Mercer (left) and Matt Busby joked with each other but there was no relenting in the game, a 2-2 draw which saw City progress 4-3 on aggregate

Manchester Evening News

The Way We Were

Every Monday and Tuesday the Manchester Evening News looks back with a nostalgic eye to The Way We Were. Each week our amazing archive photographs tell the story of how we used to live and remind us of how the world looked. Never mind the rose-tinted spectacles, look back at 'the good old days' every Monday and Tuesday in the Manchester Evening News and remember The Way We Were.

EVERY MONDAY AND TUESDAY

LOVE YOUR HISTORY?

LOVE MANCHESTER

Are you an expert on local history? Do you know the story behind things like the Manchester Ship Canal or the city's key role in the Industrial Revolution? If you have knowledge of any specific heritage subject, please get in touch and help play an important part in Britain's biggest-ever media heritage project. With your support, we will be bringing history back to life...

E-mail the Heritage Editor:

harri.aston@trinitymirror.com

LOST MANCHESTER

▶ *Caring vocation* Children's Ward at Booth Hall Children's Hospital, January 4, 1985

Caring for others at heart of NHS

From pioneering work in treating cancer to the world's first 'test tube' baby, Greater Manchester has remained at the forefront of medical breakthroughs

Greater Manchester was at the heart of the NHS when Nye Bevan launched the new service in 1948 at Park Hospital in Davyhulme, now known as Trafford General.

The region has remained at the forefront of medical breakthroughs. The Christie is famous the world over for its pioneering work in treating cancer. The first 'test tube' baby, Louise Brown, was born in Oldham in 1978.

In that same year, doctors and nurses welcomed the Queen to Withington Hospital in south Manchester. In 2012, Her Majesty chose to visit the refurbished Central Manchester hospitals as one of the first stop-offs during her Diamond Jubilee.

The Central Manchester hospitals include the new Royal Manchester Children's Hospital, opened on June 11, 2009, which has incorporated the former Royal Manchester Children's Hospital in Pendlebury and Booth Hall Children's Hospital in Blackley.

The original RMCH was founded in the mid-19th century and was the first hospital in the country to treat only children and by the time it was granted royal patronage in 1923 it was looking after around 7,000 patients every year.

The Booth Hall Children's Hospital was on Charlestown Road and was opened in 1908 by Humphrey Booth in order to care for the poor of north Manchester.

During the First World War it looked after wounded soldiers and from 1939 was prepared to take the victims of Luftwaffe air raids.

As the civilian casualties did not materialise in the numbers expected, Booth Hall welcomed children back within six months of the outbreak of war.

Both hospitals were incorporated into the newly-formed NHS.

Withington Hospital began in 1855 as the Chorlton Union workhouse. Around 10 years later, as it grew, it became the first institution to adopt a style of architecture which was said to provide a healthier design for hospitals and which was copied around England.

By 1948 it had become one of the largest general hospitals in the country. It closed its doors just after the turn of the 21st century, with services being shared across Manchester's other hospitals.

Apartments and houses now occupy the original site and Withington Community Hospital was opened further down Nell Lane at the corner with Burton Road.

▲ **Royal call** The Queen with staff at Withington Hospital during a visit to Manchester on May 5, 1982

▶ **Entertained patients** Nurse Bridie Parsey and Alison Webb, two, were entranced when characters from Alice in Wonderland visited Booth Hall Children's Hospital in December 1969

Happy child Two-year-old Stephen Gill was lost in the world of Alice in December 1969

▶ **Strange face** Stephen Gill, didn't like the look of White Rabbit played by Christopher Cook at Booth Hall in December 1969

▼ **Playful scene** March Hare (John Watts) Alice (Anne Kirksride) and Mad Hatter (David Rustidge) entertain the patients

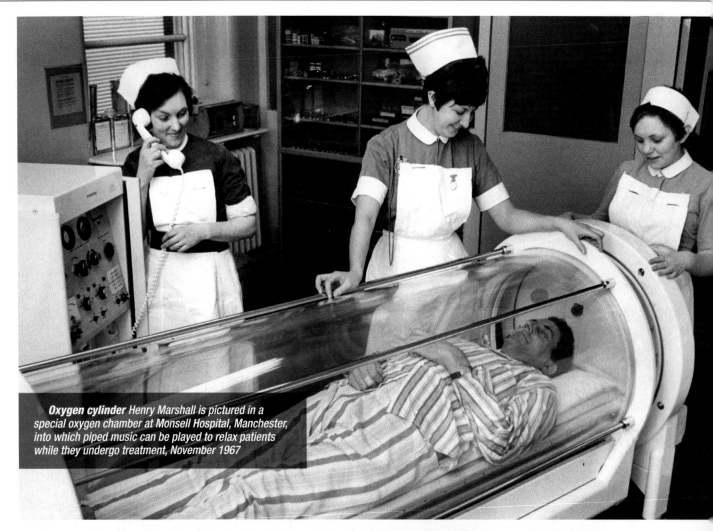

Oxygen cylinder *Henry Marshall is pictured in a special oxygen chamber at Monsell Hospital, Manchester, into which piped music can be played to relax patients while they undergo treatment, November 1967*

▶ **Service with a smile** *Women's Voluntary Service at Withington Hospital. Out-patients in the Physiotherapy Department are able to have tea while they wait for treatment in May 1959*

Star visit *Manchester United star Bobby Charlton signs an autograph for eight-year-old Billy Vickers during the team's visit to Booth Hall on November 16, 1963*

Here to help *A young boy with an injured hand gets treatment from a nurse in November 1969*

Great care *A ward in full flow at Booth Hall Children's Hospital, July 17, 1993*

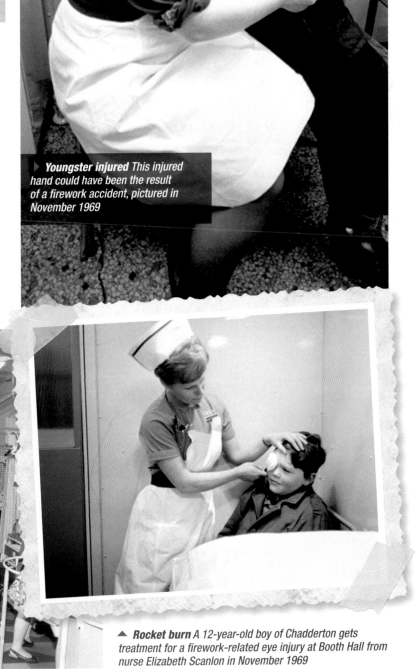

▶ **Youngster injured** *This injured hand could have been the result of a firework accident, pictured in November 1969*

▲ **Rocket burn** *A 12-year-old boy of Chadderton gets treatment for a firework-related eye injury at Booth Hall from nurse Elizabeth Scanlon in November 1969*

Congregation gathers Pope John Paul II leads a mass at Heaton Park on Monday, May 31, 1982 in front of more than 100,000 people

A Papal visit that inspired the city

When Pope John Paul II became the first Pontiff to ever visit Manchester he left a legacy and memories of a joyous visit that crossed the boundaries of religions

Heaton Park has served many purposes over the years, including a training ground for soldiers about to serve in The Great War.

As those brave men stomped around the muddy fields, they could never have known that, 70 years later, other young men would be lying on the same spot, this time on the steps of an altar, about to be ordained by His Holiness Pope John Paul II.

Pope John Paul's arrival in Heaton Park was part of the first visit to this country by a reigning Pope.

It was classified as a pastoral rather than a state visit and was therefore funded by the Catholic Church, not the Government.

On May 31, 1982 Pope John Paul met the Chief Rabbi of the United Kingdom, Sir Immanuel Jakobovits, in Prestwich before travelling to Heaton Park where he was welcomed by more than 250,000 faithful.

Many had camped for days to get a good view of the specially-constructed open-air altar, waving banners with personal greetings including 'Ow Doo John Paul'.

During the concelebrated Mass, the Pope ordained 12 men to the priesthood.

He told the new priests: "You must be men of God, his close friends. You must develop daily patterns of prayer, and penance must be a regular part of your life."

Many remember this time as a highlight in the long history of distinguished events in the city.

A few weeks after his visit, the Pope sent a telegram to Bishop Thomas Holland saying: "With many joyful memories of my visit to Britain I wish to assure you and your people of my deep appreciation of the warm welcome accorded to me in Manchester."

The historic visit is commemorated by a 16.5-tonne boulder situated in the south side of the park.

▲ **Warm welcome** Pupils at Chorlton Convent School make a banner ahead of Pope John Paul's mass at Heaton Park

II

Spiritual leader Pope John Paul II waves to the crowds in Manchester, May 1982

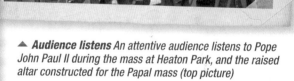

▲ **Audience listens** An attentive audience listens to Pope John Paul II during the mass at Heaton Park, and the raised altar constructed for the Papal mass (top picture)

▲ **Papal blessing** A young boy receives a blessing from the Pope during the Heaton Park mass

▶ **Great arrival** The Pope arriving at Heaton Park and being greeted by the masses of people

Manchester says hello *The congregation at the Papal mass have fun with the message of their banner*

'OW DOO JOHN PAUL

Special moment *Priests to be ordained prostrate themselves before Pope John Paul II*

▲ **Catholic leader** John Paul II was an iconic figure, much-loved throughout the world, including Manchester

▲ **Pope's blessing** Pope John Paul II descends the steps after his Heaton Park mass

◀ **Special order** Silver and gold Pope's chalice, madebysilversmith Andrew Coomber, which was used by the Pope for the mass at Heaton Park

▲ **Boisterous banners** The congregation revealed dozens of banners at Heaton Park, all welcoming Pope John Paul II to Manchester

◀ **The new generation** During the Heaton Park mass 12 priests were ordained by the Holy Father

ROTAS
OPERA
TENET
AREPO
SATOR

PATERNOSTER

▲ **Mass underway** Pope John Paul II assisted by priests, leads the Mass at Heaton Park

◀ **Memorial tree** Pope John Paul II, tree planting ahead of mass at Heaton Park

◀ **Jewish welcome** Pope John Paul II mets the Chief Rabbi of the United Kingdom, Sir Immanuel Jakobovits at the Convent of the Poor Sisters of Nazareth in Manchester

▶ **Iconic building** Free Trade Hall, on Peter Street, was designed by the Manchester-based architect Edward Walters in the 1850s, and became the first home to the Hallé Orchestra

The legendary venue that hosted the stars

Manchester's Free Trade Hall was built by public subscription and it became the people's concert hall, staging music and sporting events that thrilled the masses for generations

A Grade Two listed venue on Peter Street, the magnificent Free Trade Hall was built in 1853 on the site of the infamous Peterloo Massacre.

It was erected to commemorate the abolition of the controversial Corn Law in 1846. The council-owned building was designed by the Manchester-based architect Edward Walters and described as "the noblest monument in the Cinquecento style in England".

The Free Trade Hall, with its splendid and historic location, was an important venue for distinguished speakers including Sir Winston Churchill, who saw it as an appropriate place to address the public.

The interior needed extensive renovation after it suffered bomb damage during the Blitz and was reopened by the Queen in the early 1950s.

The Free Trade Hall had become the home of the Hallé Orchestra shortly after opening and went on to claim its place as a major influence in the popular cultural development of Manchester, with rock music cementing the venue's place in folklore.

In May 1966, Bob Dylan played his famous 'Judas' gig there during which he abandoned his acoustic guitar to play electric. This shock move prompted jeers and shouts of abuse from the audience between the songs Ballad Of A Thin Man and Like

A Rolling Stone. Pink Floyd played the Free Trade Hall five times, the Rolling Stones performed in 1971, and they were followed by Genesis two years later. Perhaps the most significant gig took place in the Lesser Free Trade Hall upstairs. In June 1976, the way was paved for the punk revolution as The Sex Pistols took to the stage.

They were supported by Manchester bands The Buzzcocks and Slaughter And The Dogs. Many famous and successful bands were formed specifically because of that one concert.

However, although the Lesser Hall had a capacity of under 100, many thousands of people have since claimed to have been in the audience and the now famous quotation from many is "I swear I was there". On a much less significant note, but no less important to many, a number of Manchester schools held their annual speech night and prize-giving events at the Free Trade Hall, which for many youngsters was their introduction to this amazing building.

It was closed by the council in 1997 and, amid much opposition principally from the Manchester Civic Society, sold to private developers after The Hallé Orchestra moved to the brand-new Bridgewater Hall.

After a £45 million redevelopment, it is now the Radisson Edwardian Hotel.

▲ **Big speech**
The Free Trade Hall is packed out as First Lord of the Admiralty Winston Churchill delivers a speech on January 27, 1940, a few months before becoming Prime Minister. In his speech, he said: "Each to our station... there is not a week, nor a day, nor an hour to be lost"

On Song
Alberto Semprini prepares to perform a piano recital at the Free Trade Hall in April 1956

▲ **Royal occasion**
The Free Trade Hall floodlit prior to the reopening by the Queen in November 1951

▲ **Wrecked**
Interior of the Free Trade Hall

▶ **Damage**
The building suffered extensive bomb damage during the Blitz

▲ **Powerful image** Arthur Sherwood Edwards working on a section of his Peterloo mural which was hung in the new Free Trade Hall, November 1951

▶ **New Era** Queen Elizabeth declares open the Free Trade Hall in Manchester, November 1951. King George VI did not attend

Civic pride *The future Queen Mother, in her role as Queen in November 1951, completes a dedication in the visitors' book at the newly-refurbished Free Trade Hall following bomb damage during the war*

Centenary celebration *George Henry Hubert Lascelles, 7th Earl of Harewood, and Countess of Harewood arrive at the recording of the Hallé Centenary Concert at the Free Trade Hall on January 30, 1958*

Big hitters A two-handed defence by Ian McKenzie, left, saves him from a right from Alf Matthews who eventually won when the referee stopped the fight in April 1964

Classic line-up Mick Jagger and Keith Richards enthrall the rock fans at the legendary venue

Hall rockers The Rolling Stones captured in their pomp at their 1971 concert

Stones fans As the Rolling Stones get ready perform on stage at the Free Trade Hall, the audience wait for the start of the legendary act in March 1971

▼ **Heavy defeat** *Jim Cooper goes down for a count of nine in the third round of his heavyweight defeat against American Chip Johnson in November 1964. Cooper retired three days later*

▼ **Down and out** *Referee signals the fight is over for Tony Barlow, known as the Manchester Midget, at the end of his fight against John McCluskey in January 1967*

◄ **Principal conductor** *The Hallé Orchestra stands to Sir John Barbirolli as he leaves the stage of the Free Trade Hall after his last performance in May 1968. He had largely saved the orchestra during the war when it had appeared it may be dissolved. On his appointment in 1943, he immediately sought to rebuild the orchestra's membership*

Childhood innocence Moss Side, October 1969 and children make the most of the autumn playing on the rubble heaps

The highs and lows of life in Moss Side

People from all over the world have come and made their home in Moss Side, the area hit by riots in the early 1980s but which these days provides one of Manchester's biggest celebrations

Incorporated into the city of Manchester in 1904, Moss Side had been a quiet, rural idyll populated by just 151 people in 1801. But by the time of its incorporation nearly 27,000 had made the area their home.

Many were Irish immigrants attracted by the promise of well-paid work and a network of neat red-bricked terraced homes had been built to accommodate this influx of people. The houses were considered better quality than those in areas such as Hulme and Chorlton-on-Medlock, and the shopping areas of Princess Road and Alexandra Road were among the busiest in the city in the early 20th century.

Manchester City FC famously made the area their home in the 1920s as Maine Road played host to some of the biggest games in the Football League, including the highest attendance in English club football history – 85,000 people packing in to watch the Sky Blues take on Stoke City in 1934.

From the 1950s, the area saw another wave of migrants, this time from the Caribbean and Africa as Britain encouraged workers to come from other parts of the Empire.

In 1960, notorious British fascist Oswald Mosely spoke at Alexandra Park in a bid to capitalise on the explosion of race riots in London. Moss Side suffered its own outbreak of violence in 1981. With youth unemployment at an all-time high and simmering resentment towards the Government, the area erupted into two days of violence in July until the police finally, and controversially, won back control.

From football to boxing, from Prince Charles to 'Prince' Naseem Hamed, Moss Side has welcomed a catalogue of famous faces to its streets over the years. Political activist and Hollywood actress Vanessa Redgrave, who founded the Workers' Revolutionary Party in the 1970s, even stood for Parliament in the Moss Side by-election of 1978. She polled just 394 votes to finish last.

These days, Moss Side provides one of the highlights of Manchester's social calendar and one of the largest celebrations of Caribbean culture in the country. The Caribbean Carnival of Manchester has been enjoyed by thousands of residents and visitors for more than three decades. Every August, Alexandra Park and surrounding streets are swamped with parades, music, dancing and other activities. The sound of steel bands, the smell of Caribbean cuisine and the party atmosphere draws everyone together.

▲ *Time of strife*
Police at the ready on Princess Road during the Moss Side riots of July 1981

◀ Destruction Broken windows and a basket of eggs thrown on the pavement outside Reid's butchers, Princess Road

▶ Wreckage Day two of the riot and the shattered remains of shops become evident on Princess Road after the violence

▼ Confrontation Police square up to local youths during the Moss Side riots

▲ Devastation Mike Gates and Francis Horn return to their Austin Allegro to find it a burnt-out wreck in Claremont Road, Rusholme

▶ **Net effect** *This youngster showed off his skills as players from the Manchester Giants basketball team paid a visit to the Chrysalis Community Project on Gooch Close in 1996*

▲ **People power** *Boxer Chris Eubank in Manchester in a bid to help the kids of Moss Side in 1993*

◀ **Royal show** *'Prince' Naseem Hamed opens the Phil Martin Centre in Moss Side in 1996. He cut the ribbon as he was watched by Phil Martin's wife, Audrey*

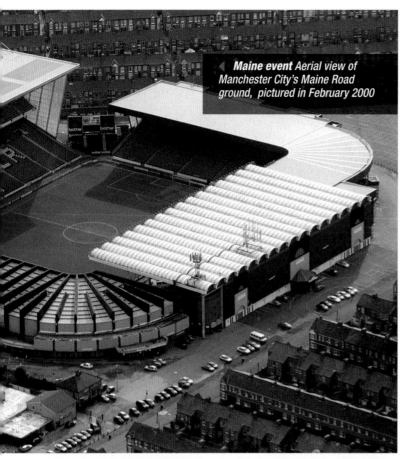

Maine event Aerial view of Manchester City's Maine Road ground, pictured in February 2000

▲ *Little and large* Ijah Cumberbatch ,11, is suitably impressed by the skills of Yorick Williams from the Manchester Giants basketball team in 1996

▲ *Smiles all round* Youngsters involved in the Chrysalis Community Project in 1996

▲ *Vibrant*
celebration
Carnival-
goers enjoy a
celebration of
Caribbean culture
at Alexandra Park
in 1978

▶ *Community*
spirit The
carnival makes
its way along
Claremont Road
undimmed
despite the
Manchester
drizzle

▲ **Music and fun** *The Caribbean carnival has become a regular and popular sight in Moss Side every year*

▲ **Fair cop** *A policeman enjoys the party atmosphere at Alexandra Park in 1973*

▶ **Wonderful creations** *The Caribbean carnival is characterised by the incredible and original designs of costumes unveiled each year*

Snow trains Railwaymen salted Manchester Victoria's pointwork so trains could access all platforms in December 1950

Trams and rail to trans-Atlantic flight

Manchester has come a long way since the earliest days of steam railways to now boasting one of Europe's biggest international airports

The control tower at Manchester Airport, pictured in May 1989

Although Manchester has boasted a number of airfields since the early 20th century, a modest stretch of land at Ringway, 10 miles south of the city, was to become one of Europe's busiest international airports.

The site, on the edge of Wythenshawe, opened in 1938 to serve growing demand and was an important training post for pilots and paratroopers during World War Two.

After the conflict, when Ringway was returned to civilian use, a new main terminal was built to cope with the boom in the British public venturing abroad as the first affordable package holidays became available.

A second runway was added in 2001 and transport bosses added a railway station. The Metrolink trams are due to run to the airport from 2015 and it will benefit from the long-term investment into high-speed rail. Manchester Airport currently serves 200 destinations and caters for around 20 million passengers each year

Before air travel became the choice for many, steam railways were king. Manchester enjoyed the first passenger railway service in the world, which ran to the neighbouring city of Liverpool and was launched in 1830.

In 1909, when Manchester United returned victorious after a 1-0 defeat of Bristol City at Wembley, the team came home by train which arrived at Great Central Station on April 25.

They were cheered by thousands of fans before taking a horse and carriage ride through the city to show off the trophy. Great Central ceased operating as a station in 1969 but remains as a Manchester landmark and is one of Europe's premier conference and event centres.

In the late 1920s and early 30s, Manchester had the second largest tramway network in the country with central and south-central Manchester districts having the largest concentration of routes. There were also extensive neighbouring systems in Salford, Oldham, Ashton & Hyde, Middleton and Rochdale.

Trolleybuses made their debut on March 1, 1938, and ran until December 31, 1966. Manchester was also served by the Ashton-under-Lyne trolleybus system, between 1925 and 1966.

Two of the former Manchester system trolley-buses are now preserved. One of them is at the Greater Manchester Transport Museum in Cheetham Hill, and the other is based at the Trolleybus Museum in Lincolnshire.

Legend returns The Flying Scotsman was repatriated from America in 1973 after being bought and rescued by Sir William McAlpine. Repatriated via Liverpool, the loco is seen at Manchester Victoria

◀ **On the road** A locomotive train is drawn through the streets of Stretford on the way to the repair shop June 1943

▼ **Planes in position** An aerial view of Manchester Airport captured in May 1989

▼ **Day and night** A doubler-decker bus in Manchester during the midday smog in November 1953

▶ **End of the road** Police Constable Gibbs of the Manchester Police is seen here on crossing patrol on the day he retired from the force in May 1952

◀ **Bumper to bumper** A view from the pavement as traffic is built up along the A556 towards Manchester, as traffic pours home from North Wales on April 7, 1969

Busy time A car park on Mosley Street, Piccadilly, September 1947

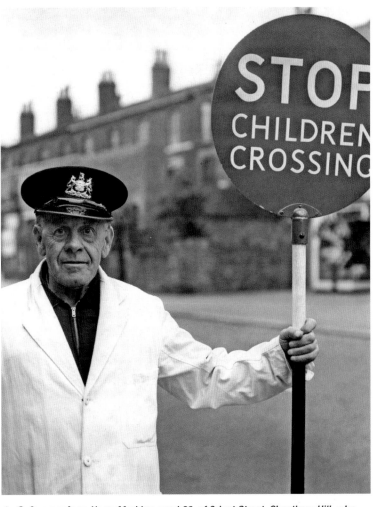

▲ *Safe crossings* Harry Markley, aged 69, of Orient Street, Cheetham Hill, who was a traffic warden on Bury Old Road, is pictured in September 1956

▶ *Tram heaven* Manchester trams line up in June 1938

▲ *Touchdown* The first BOAC Boeing 747 Jumbo jet to land at Manchester Airport in August 1970

▶ **Bright future** New buildings light up the winter nights at Salford Quays in November 2010

▶ **Grand city view** Blue skies over Manchester city centre

How we're building on a proud history

Popular culture, sport and academic excellence are just three of the elements which have contributed to the rise and rise of Manchester and its sister city, Salford

Manchester has always been recognised as one of the original modern cities. Many commentators have described it as the Workshop of the World and legendary broadcaster Tony Wilson was at pains to point out that the city has been at the forefront of three revolutions – industrial, technological and cultural.

Common threads running through the history of Manchester are vision, ambition and achievement.

Some cite the 1996 IRA bomb as a catalyst for regeneration and change. However, large-scale redevelopment had been taking place in Manchester since the early 1990s.

There was already substantial regeneration in the city centre in support of the Manchester bid for the 2000 Summer Olympics, its second Olympic bid which led directly to bringing the hugely successful Commonwealth Games to the city in 2002.

Popular culture, sport and academic excellence are just three of the elements which have contributed to the rise and rise of Manchester and its sister city, Salford.

Granada Television set the scene in the Sixties by settling in Manchester and producing iconic programmes like Coronation Street and World In Action. The BBC is continuing the tradition, having relocated many departments to Salford Quays at the newly named MediaCityUK.

The city region can justifiably claim to be the UK's music capital.

It boasts the world's most famous football clubs and is home to the university which gave society the computer.

The Manchester of the 1960s left a lot to be desired with much of the redevelopment being unpopular with residents.

Now though, the 21st century skyline is testimony to the significant change which allows the city to compete with the best from around the world.

From the pioneering Manchester Ship Canal and the docks in Salford to the ground-breaking Metrolink tram system which continues to expand; from 19th century galleries to the gleaming glass-fronted Football Museum; from disgraceful slums to modern apartments and from a Roman fort to a globally-relevant city, Manchester is a place where people choose to live and like to play.

Hugely diverse industries queue up to invest in Manchester and Salford, and it is noticeable to all that innovation is around every corner.

▲ *Modern metropolis* *An aerial view of Manchester city centre, including the massive structure of the Beetham Tower*

THE AVENUE

MediaCityUK

▲ *Striking design* Manchester can now boast some of the most exciting new structures in the whole of the country

◥ *Efficient transport* The Media City UK tram station at Salford Quays

▶ *New buildings* The Spinningfields commercial, retail and residential development

Sun shines on Manchester Spinningfields enjoys glorious weather and a chance for city dwellers to enjoy a quiet moment

Tram extension New Metrolink station on Droylsden Road, Droylsden, is unveiled on February 4, 2013

▲ **Big sky** Manchester city centre in the fading glow of a wintry sunset

New opportunities Media City at Salford Quays, where more than 1,000 BBC staff are now based

▲ **Old and new** Urbis and the Printworks at Withy Grove and Cross Street

▲ **Modern style** Salford Quays at dusk

Were you one of the millions of people who enjoyed fun-packed days out at Belle Vue? Do you remember when the Rolling Stones came to rock Free Trade Hall? Were you there when Pope John Paul II came to Manchester?

Manchester: Frame By Frame is a fascinating journey back in time revealing the magic of our city's modern history as captured through the camera lens.

Thanks to lost images newly unearthed in the Manchester Evening News and Daily Mirror archives, this special magazine shows the people and places we have known as you've never seen them before.

From royal visits and Moss Side carnivals to the Whit Walks and classic moments from thrilling City and United games, this is a glimpse inside Manchester's own private photo album.

Rare and unseen pictures of the city's famous landmarks will take you back to a bygone age and dusted down snapshots of ordinary people at work and play will remind us of the way we were.

Manchester: Frame by Frame is the first in a ground-breaking series of nostalgia magazines. This glossy publication is a must-have souvenir for anyone who has ever lived in and loved our great city.

£4.99

ISBN 978-1-908695-69-7

9 781908 695697